# Save the Florida Key Deer

# Save the
# Florida Key Deer

*Margaret Goff Clark*

COBBLEHILL BOOKS
Dutton    New York

ILLUSTRATION CREDITS

Photographs: Chas. R. Clark, 9, 15, 16, 31, 32; Key Deer Protection
Alliance, 8, 20, 23, 24, 28; LaDore Ray Kube, *ii,* 2, 4, 7, 27; Marvin
Yeomans, 19. Map on page 3 by Joseph Jakl. Cartoon on page 13
courtesy of the J. N. "Ding" Darling Foundation.

Library of Congress Cataloging-in-Publication Data
Clark, Margaret Goff.
Save the Florida Key deer / Margaret Goff Clark.
p.   cm.   Includes index.
Summary: Discusses the history, physical characteristics,
behavior, and habitat of the small deer that have lived
for hundreds of years in the Florida Keys, as well as
threats to their continued existence.
ISBN 0-525-65232-9
1. White-tailed deer—Florida—Florida Keys—Juvenile
literature. 2. Endangered species—Florida—Florida Keys—
Juvenile literature. [1. White-tailed deer. 2. Deer—Florida.
3. Endangered species.] I. Title.
QL737.U55C56  1997
333.95'9652'0975941—dc21   97-25153  CIP  AC

Published in the United States by Cobblehill Books,
an affiliate of Dutton Children's Books,
a member of Penguin Putnam Inc.
375 Hudson Street, New York, New York 10014

Designed by Mina Greenstein
Printed in Hong Kong
First Edition   10 9 8 7 6 5 4 3 2 1

To Isabel Hobba,
a personal friend for many years.
Thanks for all your help.

# Acknowledgments

I want to thank all the people who helped in the preparation of this book about the Key deer of Florida, especially the following:

DAVID S. MAEHR, former Biological Administrator of the Florida Game and Fresh Water Fish Commission, who inspired me to write about the manatee, the Florida black bear, the Florida panther, and now the Key deer;

BARRY W. STIEGLITZ, Refuge Manager, Florida Keys National Wildlife Refuges, Department of the Interior, U.S. Fish and Wildlife Service; and James Bell, interpreter, and Bill Milling, volunteer, all of whom provided resource information.

THE KEY DEER PROTECTION ALLIANCE, particularly Harold and Susan Nugent, for providing color slides as well as source material, and Robert and Brenda Schneider, for checking the manuscript for accuracy;

Louis and LaDore Ray Kube of Traverse City, Michigan, who live on Big Pine Key during the winter season and supplied many photographs;

Marvin R. Yoemans of Fort Myers, Florida, who took photographs on Big Pine Key;

Isabel Hobba for typing the manuscript;

Chas. R. Clark, my husband, who provided encouragement all the way, took many photographs, and helped pull together the final stages of the book.

# Contents

# 1

# Meet the Key Deer

Through the big window of the restaurant where I was having lunch I saw my first Key deer. Just as I had expected, it was small, about the size of a collie dog. He stood at the edge of U.S. 1, part of the Overseas Highway and the busiest road on Big Pine Key.

I dropped my sandwich onto my plate and watched the road anxiously. I knew speed limits on the Keys were strict, but many of these cars were driven by tourists who might not even notice the small, light–brown creature shifting restlessly at the edge of the road.

I heard someone behind me say, "Look at that little nuisance. Those deer don't know enough to stay out of the way of a car."

Just then the deer stepped onto the road. I leaped to my feet, ready to race out and pull it back. At the same time, two men

*Key deer crossing a highway on Big Pine Key*

came out of a store and into the road with their hands up, motioning the cars to a stop.

Calmly, the Key deer walked across the road while the cars stood still and shoppers edged the road, watching the deer.

I returned to my lunch, thinking, "These people care about their little nuisances."

FLORIDA'S LITTLE KEY DEER are gentle and likable, and move around all over the Keys they live on. The state of Florida is a peninsula jutting southward between the Atlantic Ocean and the Gulf of Mexico. The Florida Keys are a string of islands extending from the end of the peninsula in a curve to the west. They end at Key West, a popular tourist place. Since Big Pine Key is the largest and has more permanent fresh water, it attracts most of the Key deer. Many of the islands are too small to satisfy all of the deer's needs for different kinds of food and enough fresh water. Sometimes the deer swim to other islands.

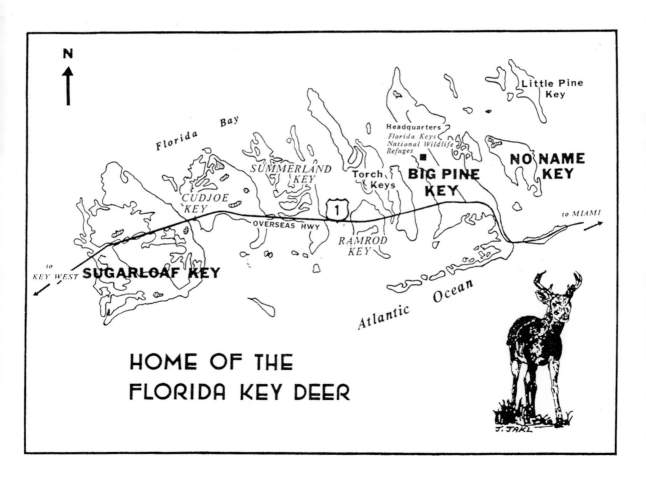

HOME OF THE
FLORIDA KEY DEER

During the daytime, Key deer wander through the towns, visiting backyards and front lawns. They nibble on the shrubs and flowers, natural foods for them. Replacing plantings can be an expense for homeowners.

*The little deer wander through backyards and front lawns.*

The deer visit the school as the children are being dismissed. The young people love the little creatures, and the deer like to share some of the remains of their lunches. There are laws against feeding the deer, but the Key deer have lost their natural fear of people, and often beg for food.

People on the Keys like the little deer, but room is scarce. The people need land for schools, stores, and houses. The deer need land with fresh water, trees and plants for food, and room for raising their fawns.

The people have looked for ways to help protect the deer. They have put up signs prohibiting fast driving. But drivers find it difficult to slow down, and road traffic kills as many as 45 Key deer every year. Deer that are hand–fed are attracted to developed areas where accidents can happen. And unnatural foods may affect the deer's behavior, appearance, and reproductive ability.

# 2

# A Bit of History

When people see the Florida Key deer for the first time, many of them think it is a large dog. Then they notice the big, upright ears and the slim legs that are too long for a dog. And then the large, dark eyes. When those eyes observe the people, the Key deer usually leaps gracefully into the air and disappears into the bush.

The small Florida Key deer live mainly on Big Pine Key and various surrounding Keys, from Little Pine Key to Sugarloaf Key. They are not found anywhere else in the world. They are a subspecies of the Virginia white–tailed deer, and the smallest of all white–tailed deer. The scientific name for them is *Odocoileus virginianus clavium*.

An adult doe stands about 24 inches high at the shoulder. Bucks are slightly taller, with a shoulder height as much as 30 inches.

*A Key deer is light brown with the underpart white. The underside of the fluffy tail is also white.*

Does weigh from 45 to 65 pounds, while bucks weigh as much as 55 to 80 pounds. The upper part of the deer's body is light brown. The underpart is white, and so is the underside of its fluffy tail.

The Florida Key deer is an endangered species. It was declared endangered under the 1967 Endangered Species Preservation Act passed by Congress. There are only 250 to 300 of these deer left. Since they roam over many Keys, it is impossible to make a perfect count, but in the 1970s the U.S. Fish and Wildlife Service reported 400 Key deer, a figure that has never since been surpassed.

There is no record of how the deer came to the Keys. It is believed that thousands of years ago there was a long peninsula extending south from the Florida mainland and this area eventually became the Keys. When the earth became warmer about

*The Key deer has been called "a great wonder."*

*Key deer thrive on the natural plants and grasses of the Florida Keys.*

10,000 years ago, the glaciers and polar ice caps began to melt. The oceans rose higher and broke up Florida's peninsula into many islands.

It is assumed that the Key deer migrated from the Florida mainland across that peninsula. When the peninsula broke up, the deer were stranded, too far from the Florida mainland to swim back to it.

The first reported sighting of Key deer was from a crewman on one of Christopher Columbus's ships. It was recorded in the ship's log. Columbus set sail for his fourth and last voyage in May, 1502, so the Key deer must have been on the Keys then.

Another report came from a Spanish shipwreck victim, Escalante Fontaneda, who kept a diary during his seventeen years of imprisonment by the Calusa Indians of Florida. In his recording of the Key deer, he called it a "great wonder." He was there in 1575.

These early records from the past prove the early residence of the Key deer on the Florida Keys. The islands were their home. At first, there were probably few humans, if any, on the Keys. Then the Calusa Indians, who lived in Florida, found their way to the Keys and encountered the deer living there. The deer could survive on the grasses, on plants and leaves of the white and red mangrove trees, and on berries. They had no large enemies, which meant that there was no need to grow tall and strong, or to have long legs to fight with or to protect themselves by running away. The only creature they might fear was the rattlesnake.

The Calusa Indians killed some of the deer, but took only as many as they needed to use for food and clothing. When pioneer settlers came, they almost wiped out the Key deer, killing them not only for food, but for pleasure. Although the deer were small, they were sturdy enough to keep their species alive.

Today, survival of the Key deer in the wild depends on it having enough land and space. Both the people of the Keys and the Key deer must adjust to the limited habitat available. Both are involved in a continuing challenge. Can the deer adapt once again, with the help of people who care about them?

# 3

# The Key Deer Refuge

In 1934, famous cartoonist Jay N. "Ding" Darling drew a picture of men and dogs hunting Key deer in Florida. He called them "toy" deer, and his cartoon was published in newspapers across the country. It stirred up support for the Key deer, but it did not put a stop to the hunting.

Florida's legislature banned Key deer hunting in 1939, but the killing went on, and the herd decreased to less than 100 animals by the late 1940s.

In 1947, an eleven–year–old boy named Glenn Allen of Miami noticed this tiny animal that appeared and then seemed to disappear. As time went on, Glenn could see that it was in trouble. He decided to try to find help.

Wanting to go to the highest source, he wrote to President Harry Truman and later to President Dwight Eisenhower. In his

*The 1934 "Ding" Darling cartoon called attention to the little deer on the Florida Keys.*

letters he suggested that the government set aside land for what seemed to be a vanishing species. His classmates and Boy Scout troops also wrote letters.

Congress did not take action immediately. There was local opposition to using land for a wildlife refuge. Property owners did not want their land taken for this use. Also, hunters saw no reason for their sport to be spoiled.

United States congressmen from Florida repeatedly introduced legislation to provide the Key deer with a permanent home. Poachers were their worst enemy, and by 1950 there were only about fifty deer left. Fortunately, Jack Watson was their best friend. As an agent for the U.S. Fish and Wildlife Service in 1946, part of his job was to patrol the Keys.

Watson was a big, gentle man who cared for people and all creatures in need, but he could be tough on anyone who was abusing nature. His solitary and fearless efforts against poachers got results. Overcoming multitudes of mosquitoes and the ever–present danger of poisonous snakes, Watson tracked down illegal hunters and brought them to justice.

Besides being an officer of the law, Watson educated the public about the Key deer and other wildlife. His efforts resulted in broad public support for the unusual beauty of nature and creatures on the Keys. He was called "the man who saved the Key deer." In a Monroe County publication, entitled *The Monroe County Environmental Story,* there is a photograph of Jack Watson being kissed on the ear by a Key deer. (Monroe County takes in the Florida Keys.)

The National Key Deer Refuge became a fact in 1957. In 1967, the Key deer was declared to be an endangered species, which means that it is in danger of becoming extinct. It also means that it is entitled to have the protection of the United States government. The hopes of Glenn Allen had finally come true.

THE KEY DEER REFUGE, covering more than 8,000 acres, is part of the National Wildlife Refuge System. Much of the refuge land

*The National Key Deer Refuge was established in 1957.*

is separated by expanses of water, some of which is too deep to wade and the deer must swim to get from one island to another.

The refuge is available to the deer at all times. If any animal needs care, day or night, someone is there to care for it. But the refuge is closed to people at night to give the animals a chance to rest and be alone.

The National Wildlife Refuge System maintains refuges for a number of animals in Florida. Those that are located along the north–south bird flyways have arranged to provide places where the birds can rest and eat. Every refuge is different and takes care of different needs of the animals protected there. Some wild areas

*Key deer grazing at a water hole on No Name Key. The deer need fresh water and natural plants to eat.*

did not need any changes to become suitable as refuges. The burning of woody undergrowth in the National Key Deer Refuge helped the growth of the tender shoots that Key deer eat.

Besides keeping wild lands for animals and birds, the refuge managers make it possible for people to see natural beauty, to learn about the plants and animals in the refuge, and to enjoy hiking, bird watching, photography. There are regulations for the benefit of both people and wildlife: hiking only on designated trails, no camping on refuge lands, no fires allowed. Airboats, hovercraft, and waterskiing are not allowed, and feeding or molesting wildlife or removing plantlife is prohibited.

Florida refuges protect marsh rabbits, silver rice rats, the eastern diamondback rattlesnake, alligators, great white heron, ospreys, and other species, as well as a variety of plantlife. Managers plan and work toward ways to save the wilderness that for years had been devoured by cities and roads and factories. The refuges are helping to save the wilderness for all of us.

# 4

# A Key Deer's Life

Although four seasons are most common in the rest of North America, the Florida Keys have only two. There is a dry season from November through April when little rain falls. May to October is the rainy season, with storms that build up and bring plenty of rain to the Keys.

Because of their geographic location just north of the Tropics, a tropical maritime climate prevails, providing a breeding ground for American crocodiles, as well as alligators. Other land and water animals include raccoons, mice and rats, box turtles, lizards, and many different kinds of snakes. Nesting in the trees are white-crowned pigeons and mockingbirds. Ibis, egrets, hawks, and heron are common transitory birds.

During the dry season the Key deer sometimes go into the sea, to swim to another island which might have fresh water holes.

Some outlying islands have water holes built especially for Key deer by National Key Deer Refuge volunteers.

Big Pine Key has fresh water the year around. During the rainy season, storms fill holes in the rocky limestone base that forms the islands. They provide the little deer with fresh water to drink, although they can tolerate a certain amount of salt.

The Key deer also have two seasons. The breeding season begins in November and continues through December. Generally, the bucks are solitary creatures and keep to themselves. During the nonbreeding season, two or three of them will feed and bed together. Adult males often have a range of 300 acres, while adult females range over approximately 130 acres.

*A buck's antlers grow to full size before he scrapes off the velvet.*

When the three–year–old buck's antlers have grown, he scrapes off the velvet covers, displaying full–sized, well–polished antlers. Now he is prepared to fight for the perfect doe. Not all male deer have to fight for a mate, though. Smaller bucks sometimes step aside and wait for a lone doe.

A buck seeking a mate has no time for anything but the doe he is following. Wherever the doe leads, he will follow. Younger, inexperienced bucks can get into trouble with him then. The older buck will not let any other male near the doe he wants.

The big buck himself is sometimes in danger. When he is following a doe's scent, he can be blind to a coming car, or he may not notice a "mosquito ditch" until he has fallen into it.

*A buck will fight to get the doe he wants for a mate.*

When bucks want the same doe, they face each other like two boxers and fight, while the doe watches. But they do not fight with anything as soft as boxers' gloves. Their weapons are their antlers and sharp hooves.

Often they push with their antlers held in front like shields. Sometimes they wound each other, but at times the weaker one just gives up and walks away, leaving the stronger deer to mate with the doe. This natural process ensures that the stronger deer will be the father of the fawns.

# 5

# Key Deer Fawns

During April and May most of the young fawns are born, before the rainy season starts and after the doe's 204–day gestation period. Does usually don't breed until about two years old.

Before the fawn arrives, the doe goes into the pinelands forest to find a cool, sheltered place where the baby will be safe and hidden from human contact. She needs fresh water, too. There she has a fawn or perhaps two. First–time mothers usually have only a single fawn, but occasionally older does have twins. However, Key deer have fewer twins than the larger white–tailed deer.

The doe greets the fawn by licking it all over. Fawns weigh two to four pounds, and their coats are reddish brown with white spots on their backs. More male fawns than female fawns are born.

The fawns are more alert than human babies. Their eyes are open, and soon they can walk a little and quickly find the mother's milk. Does have udders with four nipples like a cow. When the fawns have nursed until they are full, they lie down

*Fawns are reddish brown with white spots on their backs.*

*Most fawns are born in April and May.*

among the bushes and go to sleep. Then the mother goes off to
eat, to make more milk for her baby. She grazes on the grass and
browses on leaves, and eats any fruit she can find.

The doe is a good mother. During the day she rests near the
place where the fawn is hidden. Its spotted coat helps to hide it.
Every little while the doe goes to feed her baby. When it is old
enough to go with her, she teaches it what foods to eat and where
to find fresh water in the holes in the rock.

The doe walks in front of the fawn and raises her fluffy white tail like a flag as a signal when there is danger ahead. She also teaches it to hide when people or other animals come near. Unfortunately, they forget this when people feed them.

When the fawn is six weeks old, the doe joins a group of other adult females and their fawns. The does look after each other's babies. Later, when the fawns have babies, too, they all are welcomed into the family group.

Sometimes the fawn has a short life.  From the time it is born it faces several dangers. A number of deer are killed each year by road traffic. If a newborn wanders away from its mother, it may fall into a canal or a mosquito ditch. Water three feet deep is deep enough to drown a fawn. Free–roaming dogs often chase after and kill the tiny deer, too.

The fawn's life is not all sad, though. The mother and baby play together. To teach it what to eat, she leans over the fawn as she is chewing. The fawn sniffs the mother's mouth and learns what food is good to eat. Although most Key deer live only eight or nine years, one female lived to be twenty–one years old.

Concerned people are working to make life easier for the Key deer, and they are making progress. But all improvement takes money, and that is scarce. One of the greatest needs of the Key deer is land where they can live in safety from cars, roving dogs, or humans.

# 6

# Some Key Deer Troubles

Hunters were not the only enemies of the little Key deer. Rainstorms that brought the water they needed sometimes were so strong they drowned the deer. People who moved into the Keys thought the gentle and lovable little deer were pests and killed them for food or amusement.

Sometimes a free–roaming dog, one that is not on a leash and is not confined to a yard, chases a deer into the road where it may be hit by a car.

When people began to know the little deer, they wanted to help them in many different ways. Even a dog did his best.

One morning at 2:30 A.M., the barking of a twelve–year–old Brittany spaniel named Pi–Wacket aroused the owner of the dog and a neighbor. The two men hurried out to discover what had upset the dog. They soon found that a young fawn had tumbled off the bank of a canal and was struggling to keep its head above water. The men grabbed the soaking wet fawn and wrapped it in a blanket.

A few minutes later, they saw a doe on a nearby lawn. The men walked toward the doe, unwrapped the little fawn and put it down. The mother and baby went to each other and at once the fawn started to nurse. Then the doe and her fawn moved away into the bush.

The dog's owner was quoted as saying, "It was the dog that saved that little deer. He's a trained bird dog and he doesn't chase deer."

*A Key deer grazing along a roadside.*

*Biologists can keep track of deer movements by using a radio collar.*

ANOTHER KEY DEER, a fawn, seemed to have no fear of people or cars. The schoolchildren loved her and began to call her "Pine Needles." Perhaps this was because she lived on Big Pine Key.

Pine Needles was only a few months old when she was struck by a car. Her head was injured and she had broken legs. She was so badly hurt that the Refuge Manager and veterinarians who took care of her could not believe that she would live. To their surprise and joy, she showed a strong determination to stay alive.

Pine Needles was driven to Metrozoo in Dade County and then flown to the University of Florida to give her the best treatment available, as is always done for injured Key deer. Wherever Pine Needles went, she won the hearts and admiration of all.

When at last she was returned to Big Pine Key, refuge workers tried to teach her to be a deer again and not a pet. They brought wild Key deer to the refuge and tried to cure her dependence on people.

Finally, they put a radio collar on her neck and released Pine Needles in a woodland area of Big Pine Key where she would not see people or even hear cars. Biologists constantly kept track of her. With the help of the radio collar, they followed her movements as she walked around her native island, eating and drinking.

For a few weeks a steady beep came from her collar. Then suddenly the radio signal was beeping faster. That meant she was not moving. With the help of the radio signal, they found her body about a mile from where they had released her.

No one knew what killed Pine Needles because vultures had reached her first. There were no clues as to what happened to her.

The people on Big Pine Key and everyone who had known her grieved for little Pine Needles. "The deer's life was not wasted," said one of the men who cared for her. He said he was even more convinced that breeding or keeping Key deer in captivity is a mistake. "Later, they cannot adapt to a wild environment. There are things that deer teach to each other as they're growing that this little deer never got to learn."

# 7

# What About the Future?

The majority of Key deer live on Big Pine Key. This Key has more fresh water the year around than the other Keys. It also has many healthful plants and fruits that the deer need and like. That is why most Key deer live on Big Pine Key.

This Key also has handsome trees, colorful flowers, sandy beaches, and a road that leads directly to the mainland of Florida. These are some of the reasons why people came to Big Pine Key to live.

The Key deer have lived on Big Pine Key for thousands of years, and grew healthy and strong on the natural foods. They eat more than 160 different plants, including red mangrove, black mangrove, Indian mulberry, silver palm, and grasses.

Now the deer like people food. This never is as good for the deer as its natural diet. Besides, it makes the deer unafraid of peo-

ple, and of cars. Hand–feeding the deer is punishable by a $250
fine. Signs that say "Unlawful to feed Key deer" have been put
up, but when deer wander through the small towns, they can
usually find handouts or garbage.

In 1996, as many as 104 Key deer were lost. Two–thirds of those
that died were killed by cars. The deer wander along the high-
ways in search of food. Signs that say "Drive with caution. You
are entering an Endangered Species area. Please protect the Key
deer" have been put up. But drivers often have trouble seeing
and avoiding the tiny deer, even when obeying the 30 to 35 miles

*Feeding the Key deer is not good for them and is prohibited.*

*"Drive with caution" signs are put up to protect the Key deer.*

an hour speed limits. The Key Deer Protection Alliance advises drivers to "drive deerfensively."

Also, be alert for the deer. Know the coloring of Key deer. If you want to take a photograph, pull off the road to do so.

HOW CAN THE KEY DEER BE SAVED? The National Key Deer Refuge has helped, but more land is needed. The building of housing developments on the Keys has caused conflict between the people living there and those concerned with protecting the Key deer. On Big Pine Key, an island two miles wide and eight miles long, there are severe restrictions on construction of new homes, schools, and roads because the Key deer is an endangered species. But owners denied the right to build are unhappy.

The National Wildlife Federation's policy today is designed to protect the Key deer and other wildlife while also providing a quality environment for humans. Hopefully, the future will see people and deer both having space enough on the Florida Keys. The little deer are found nowhere else in the world. Florida's "toy" deer must not disappear.

# *For More Information*

If you care about the Key deer of Florida and would like to know more about them and what you can do to see that they are protected, contact the following:

Refuge Manager
National Key Deer Refuge
U.S. Fish and Wildlife Service
P. O. Box 430510
Big Pine Key, Florida 33043-0510
(305) 872–2239
(305) 872-3675 (FAX)

Key Deer Protection Alliance
P. O. Box 430224
Big Pine Key, Florida 33043-0224
(305) 872-3509

# Index